EMMANUEL JOSEPH

The Courage to Command, Public Speaking, Leadership, and the Power of Action in Relationships

Copyright © 2025 by Emmanuel Joseph

All rights reserved. No part of this publication may be reproduced, stored or transmitted in any form or by any means, electronic, mechanical, photocopying, recording, scanning, or otherwise without written permission from the publisher. It is illegal to copy this book, post it to a website, or distribute it by any other means without permission.

First edition

This book was professionally typeset on Reedsy.
Find out more at reedsy.com

Contents

1. Chapter 1: Finding Your Voice — 1
2. Chapter 2: The Anatomy of Leadership — 3
3. Chapter 3: The Art of Persuasion — 4
4. Chapter 4: Building Trust — 5
5. Chapter 5: The Power of Nonverbal Communication — 6
6. Chapter 6: Leading with Empathy — 7
7. Chapter 7: The Courage to Act — 8
8. Chapter 8: The Importance of Vision — 9
9. Chapter 9: Fostering Collaboration — 10
10. Chapter 10: Navigating Conflict — 11
11. Chapter 11: The Role of Accountability — 12
12. Chapter 12: The Power of Recognition — 13
13. Chapter 13: Leading Through Change — 14
14. Chapter 14: Developing Future Leaders — 15
15. Chapter 15: The Impact of Culture — 16
16. Chapter 16: The Balance of Work and Life — 17
17. Chapter 17: The Legacy of Leadership — 18

1

Chapter 1: Finding Your Voice

P ublic speaking demands more than just vocal skills; it's about tapping into your authentic self. As a leader, your voice becomes the beacon that guides, inspires, and reassures others. In a world full of distractions, finding your voice means embracing your unique perspective and speaking with conviction. This authenticity connects deeply with your audience, fostering trust and admiration.

Understanding your values and beliefs is crucial in mustering the courage to speak up. When you are passionate about your message, your words carry weight, and your audience senses your sincerity. The journey to finding your voice involves introspection and self-awareness. It's about aligning your speech with your inner convictions, making your communication powerful and genuine.

Public speaking is not merely about delivering information; it's about storytelling. By sharing personal anecdotes and experiences, you add a layer of relatability to your speech. Stories captivate your audience and make your message memorable. The ability to weave narratives into your speech is a hallmark of effective public speaking.

Lastly, practice is key. Rehearse your speeches to gain confidence and refine your delivery. Seek feedback and continuously improve. Finding your voice is an ongoing process that evolves with experience and reflection. Embrace this journey, and your voice will become a powerful tool in your leadership arsenal.

2

Chapter 2: The Anatomy of Leadership

True leadership transcends titles and positions; it's about actions and influence. At its core, leadership is about serving others and helping them reach their full potential. This chapter delves into the anatomy of leadership, examining the qualities that define a great leader. These qualities include empathy, integrity, resilience, and vision.

Empathy allows leaders to connect with their team on a personal level, fostering trust and collaboration. Integrity ensures that leaders are consistent and trustworthy in their actions. Resilience helps leaders navigate challenges and setbacks with grace. Vision provides a clear direction and inspires others to follow.

Cultivating these qualities requires intentional practice and self-reflection. Leaders must continually assess their strengths and areas for improvement. By embracing vulnerability and being open to growth, leaders can enhance their effectiveness and inspire their team.

Leadership is not a solitary journey. It involves building strong relationships and empowering others. Great leaders invest in their team's development, providing guidance and support. They create an environment where everyone feels valued and motivated to contribute their best.

3

Chapter 3: The Art of Persuasion

Persuasion is a powerful tool in a leader's arsenal. It's not about manipulating or coercing others, but about presenting ideas in a compelling way that resonates with your audience. This chapter explores the principles of persuasive communication, including ethos, pathos, and logos.

Ethos refers to building credibility. A leader's integrity and expertise establish trust with the audience. Pathos involves connecting emotionally, appealing to the audience's values and desires. Logos is about presenting logical arguments supported by evidence and reason.

Understanding these principles enables leaders to craft messages that influence and inspire. Persuasion also involves active listening. By understanding the audience's perspective and addressing their concerns, leaders can build rapport and gain support.

However, persuasion should always be ethical. It's about empowering others to make informed decisions, not manipulating them for personal gain. Ethical persuasion fosters long-term trust and respect.

In practice, persuasion involves storytelling, analogies, and rhetorical questions. These techniques engage the audience and make the message more relatable. By mastering the art of persuasion, leaders can drive positive change and inspire action.

4

Chapter 4: Building Trust

Trust is the foundation of any successful relationship, whether personal or professional. As a leader, building trust with your team, stakeholders, and community is paramount. This chapter examines the elements of trust, including reliability, transparency, and authenticity.

Reliability means consistently delivering on promises and meeting expectations. Transparency involves being open and honest in communication, even when delivering bad news. Authenticity is about being genuine and true to oneself, which fosters deeper connections.

Leaders demonstrate trustworthiness through their actions and decisions. They show commitment to their team's well-being and success. By acknowledging mistakes and learning from them, leaders build credibility and respect.

The impact of trust on team dynamics and performance is profound. A high-trust environment encourages collaboration, innovation, and risk-taking. Team members feel safe to express ideas and concerns, leading to better problem-solving and creativity.

Rebuilding trust when it has been broken requires patience and effort. Leaders must acknowledge the breach, apologize sincerely, and take corrective actions. Consistent effort to rebuild trust can restore relationships and strengthen the team.

5

Chapter 5: The Power of Nonverbal Communication

While words are essential, nonverbal cues often speak louder. From body language to facial expressions, nonverbal communication plays a critical role in how leaders are perceived. This chapter delves into the various aspects of nonverbal communication and how leaders can use them to reinforce their message.

Techniques for projecting confidence, empathy, and authority through nonverbal cues are invaluable. For instance, maintaining eye contact can demonstrate confidence and sincerity, while a firm handshake can convey strength and reliability. Being mindful of your posture, gestures, and facial expressions can significantly enhance your communication effectiveness.

Mastering nonverbal communication also involves being perceptive to others' nonverbal signals. Understanding your audience's body language can provide insights into their reactions and emotions. This awareness allows leaders to adjust their approach and foster a more engaging and responsive interaction.

By practicing and refining these skills, leaders can cultivate a commanding presence that resonates with their audience. Nonverbal communication is not just about being expressive; it's about creating a genuine connection that transcends words.

6

Chapter 6: Leading with Empathy

Empathy is the ability to understand and share the feelings of others. It's a vital skill for leaders who want to connect with their team and create a supportive work environment. This chapter explores the role of empathy in leadership, including how it fosters trust, collaboration, and innovation.

Developing empathy requires active listening and being fully present in conversations. Leaders can show empathy by acknowledging others' perspectives and emotions, asking open-ended questions, and validating their experiences. Empathy builds a sense of belonging and encourages open communication within the team.

Empathetic leaders are better equipped to address conflicts and challenges constructively. By understanding the underlying emotions and motivations, they can facilitate resolutions that are fair and considerate. This approach not only strengthens relationships but also enhances team morale and productivity.

Empathy is not a one-time effort but a continuous practice. Leaders who consistently demonstrate empathy create a positive and inclusive culture. This environment promotes mutual respect and empowers individuals to contribute their best, driving collective success.

7

Chapter 7: The Courage to Act

Leadership requires courage – the courage to make difficult decisions, take risks, and stand up for what's right. This chapter examines the different types of courage leaders must embody, from moral and intellectual courage to emotional and social courage.

Moral courage involves making ethical decisions, even when they are unpopular or challenging. Intellectual courage is about embracing new ideas and perspectives, while emotional courage pertains to being vulnerable and authentic. Social courage requires leaders to advocate for others and champion diversity and inclusion.

Real-life examples of courageous leadership illustrate the impact it can have on organizations and communities. These stories inspire leaders to take bold actions and persevere in the face of adversity. Courageous leadership drives progress and fosters a culture of resilience and innovation.

Building and sustaining courage involves self-reflection and a commitment to personal growth. Leaders can develop courage by setting clear values, seeking feedback, and learning from failures. Courage is not the absence of fear but the willingness to act despite it, creating a lasting positive influence.

8

Chapter 8: The Importance of Vision

A compelling vision is a leader's roadmap to the future. It provides direction, motivation, and a sense of purpose. This chapter explores the importance of vision in leadership, including how to craft a clear and inspiring vision statement.

An effective vision captures the essence of what an organization aspires to achieve. It aligns with the core values and goals, guiding decision-making and actions. Leaders must articulate their vision clearly and passionately to inspire and rally their team.

Communicating the vision involves storytelling and creating a shared sense of purpose. Leaders should engage their team in the vision-setting process, allowing them to contribute ideas and feel ownership. This collaborative approach fosters commitment and enthusiasm.

Aligning the vision with organizational goals and values ensures consistency and coherence. Leaders must regularly revisit and refine the vision to stay relevant and responsive to changing circumstances. A well-communicated vision empowers the team to work towards a common goal with dedication and unity.

9

Chapter 9: Fostering Collaboration

Collaboration is key to achieving collective success. As a leader, fostering a collaborative environment involves encouraging open communication, promoting diversity of thought, and creating opportunities for team members to contribute and shine. This chapter delves into the benefits of collaboration and practical strategies for fostering it within your team.

Creating a culture of collaboration starts with open communication. Leaders must encourage team members to share their ideas and opinions freely. This involves active listening and creating a safe space where everyone feels valued. Open communication fosters trust and ensures that diverse perspectives are considered.

Promoting diversity of thought is essential for innovation and problem-solving. Leaders should seek out and value different viewpoints, encouraging team members to challenge assumptions and think creatively. Embracing diversity leads to more robust and well-rounded solutions.

Creating opportunities for team members to contribute and shine involves recognizing and leveraging their unique strengths. Leaders can assign roles and responsibilities based on individual skills and interests, providing opportunities for professional growth and development. This approach not only enhances team performance but also boosts morale and engagement.

10

Chapter 10: Navigating Conflict

Conflict is an inevitable part of any relationship, but how leaders handle it can make or break their effectiveness. This chapter explores the dynamics of conflict and provides tools for navigating it constructively. Leaders must understand the root causes of conflict and address them proactively.

Different conflict resolution styles and techniques, such as mediation and negotiation, are essential tools for leaders. Mediation involves facilitating a dialogue between conflicting parties to reach a mutually beneficial solution. Negotiation requires finding common ground and making compromises to resolve disputes.

Addressing underlying issues is crucial for lasting resolution. Leaders must dig deeper to understand the emotions and motivations driving the conflict. This involves asking probing questions and empathetic listening. By addressing the root causes, leaders can prevent conflicts from recurring.

Promoting healthy dialogue and turning conflict into an opportunity for growth involves fostering a culture of feedback and continuous improvement. Leaders should encourage team members to express their concerns constructively and view conflicts as learning experiences. This approach strengthens relationships and enhances team cohesion.

11

Chapter 11: The Role of Accountability

Accountability is crucial for building trust and ensuring that goals are met. Leaders must hold themselves and their team members accountable for their actions and performance. This chapter examines the role of accountability in leadership, including how to establish clear expectations, provide constructive feedback, and create a culture of accountability.

Establishing clear expectations involves setting specific, measurable, achievable, relevant, and time-bound (SMART) goals. Leaders must communicate these expectations clearly and ensure that team members understand their responsibilities. Clear expectations provide a roadmap for success and minimize misunderstandings.

Providing constructive feedback is essential for performance improvement. Leaders should deliver feedback promptly, focusing on specific behaviors and outcomes. Positive feedback reinforces desired behaviors, while constructive feedback highlights areas for improvement and offers actionable suggestions.

Creating a culture of accountability involves fostering a sense of ownership and responsibility among team members. Leaders can achieve this by leading by example, recognizing and rewarding accountability, and addressing issues promptly. A culture of accountability promotes transparency, trust, and high performance.

Chapter 12: The Power of Recognition

Recognizing and celebrating achievements is a powerful way to motivate and inspire others. This chapter explores the importance of recognition in leadership, including how to provide meaningful and timely recognition. Leaders must understand the impact of recognition on team morale and performance.

Different forms of recognition, from verbal praise and awards to more personalized gestures, can make a significant difference. Verbal praise during team meetings or written commendations can boost morale and reinforce positive behaviors. Personalized gestures, such as handwritten notes or small tokens of appreciation, show genuine appreciation and strengthen relationships.

Providing timely recognition is crucial for maximizing its impact. Leaders should acknowledge achievements as soon as possible to reinforce the behavior and maintain motivation. Delayed recognition can diminish its effectiveness and may be perceived as insincere.

By acknowledging the contributions and efforts of others, leaders can boost morale, strengthen relationships, and foster a positive organizational culture. Recognition creates a sense of belonging and motivates team members to continue striving for excellence.

13

Chapter 13: Leading Through Change

Change is a constant in today's fast-paced world, and leaders must be adept at navigating and managing it. This chapter explores the challenges and opportunities of leading through change. Leaders must understand the stages of change and the emotional responses associated with it.

The stages of change include awareness, interest, evaluation, trial, and adoption. Leaders must guide their team through each stage, addressing concerns and providing support. Communication and transparency are crucial for managing change effectively.

Building resilience and adaptability involves fostering a growth mindset and encouraging continuous learning. Leaders can support their team by providing resources and training to develop new skills. Creating a culture of continuous improvement helps teams adapt to change and stay competitive.

Supporting the team through change involves empathy and understanding. Leaders should acknowledge the emotional impact of change and provide reassurance. By fostering a supportive environment, leaders can help their team navigate change successfully and embrace new opportunities.

14

Chapter 14: Developing Future Leaders

Great leaders invest in developing the next generation of leaders. This chapter examines the importance of leadership development and provides practical strategies for mentoring and coaching others. Effective leadership development is essential for the long-term success and sustainability of any organization.

Identifying potential leaders within your team involves recognizing qualities such as initiative, adaptability, and a willingness to learn. Leaders should provide opportunities for growth by assigning challenging projects and encouraging team members to take on new responsibilities. This approach helps individuals build confidence and develop their skills.

Creating development plans tailored to each individual's strengths and aspirations is crucial. These plans should include specific goals, resources, and timelines for achieving them. Regular check-ins and feedback sessions help track progress and ensure that development goals are met.

Mentoring and coaching are powerful tools for leadership development. Mentors provide guidance, support, and valuable insights based on their experience. Coaches help individuals identify their strengths and areas for improvement, set goals, and develop action plans. By investing time and effort in developing future leaders, organizations can create a strong leadership pipeline and ensure continued success.

15

Chapter 15: The Impact of Culture

Organizational culture plays a significant role in shaping behavior and performance. This chapter explores the impact of culture on leadership and provides insights into how leaders can influence and shape it. A healthy organizational culture promotes trust, collaboration, and innovation.

Leaders must lead by example, embodying the values and behaviors they wish to see in their team. This involves demonstrating integrity, empathy, and accountability in their actions. By modeling these behaviors, leaders set the standard for others to follow.

Aligning the culture with organizational values and goals ensures consistency and coherence. Leaders should communicate the organization's mission and values clearly and consistently. This helps create a shared sense of purpose and direction, guiding decision-making and actions.

Creating a positive and inclusive culture involves fostering open communication, recognizing and celebrating achievements, and promoting diversity and inclusion. Leaders should encourage team members to share their ideas and opinions, creating a sense of belonging and engagement. By cultivating a healthy culture, leaders can enhance team performance and drive organizational success.

16

Chapter 16: The Balance of Work and Life

Finding a balance between work and personal life is essential for long-term success and well-being. This chapter examines the challenges leaders face in achieving work-life balance and provides practical strategies for managing it. A healthy work-life balance promotes productivity, creativity, and overall well-being.

Setting boundaries is crucial for maintaining work-life balance. Leaders should establish clear limits on working hours and prioritize time for personal activities and self-care. This involves delegating tasks effectively and avoiding overcommitment.

Prioritizing self-care is essential for sustaining energy and focus. Leaders should make time for activities that promote physical, mental, and emotional well-being, such as exercise, hobbies, and relaxation. Self-care helps prevent burnout and ensures that leaders are at their best.

Creating a supportive work environment involves promoting flexibility and understanding. Leaders should encourage their team to prioritize work-life balance and provide the necessary resources and support. By modeling work-life balance and supporting their team, leaders can create a healthier and more sustainable approach to work.

17

Chapter 17: The Legacy of Leadership

A leader's legacy is defined by the lasting impact they have on others. This chapter explores the concept of legacy in leadership, including how to create a positive and enduring legacy. A meaningful legacy is built on values, actions, and the difference made in the lives of others.

Living your values is essential for creating a positive legacy. Leaders should consistently demonstrate their principles and beliefs through their actions and decisions. This integrity inspires trust and respect, leaving a lasting impression on those they lead.

Making a difference involves contributing to the growth and development of others. Leaders should invest in their team's success, providing guidance, support, and opportunities for growth. By helping others achieve their potential, leaders create a ripple effect that extends beyond their immediate influence.

Reflecting on and celebrating your leadership journey is an important part of legacy building. Leaders should take time to acknowledge their achievements, learn from their experiences, and continue growing and evolving. By embracing continuous improvement and staying true to their values, leaders can leave a lasting and positive legacy.

"**The Courage to Command: Public Speaking, Leadership, and the Power of Action in Relationships**" is a comprehensive guide designed for anyone looking to enhance their leadership skills and command respect

CHAPTER 17: THE LEGACY OF LEADERSHIP

in various aspects of life. This book delves into the essential qualities and techniques that define effective leadership, from finding your unique voice and mastering public speaking to fostering trust and collaboration within your team.

Through seventeen insightful chapters, you'll explore the art of persuasion, the importance of empathy, and the power of nonverbal communication. You'll learn how to navigate conflict, build accountability, and lead through change. Each chapter is filled with practical strategies, real-life examples, and actionable advice to help you develop the courage to act and inspire others.

Whether you're a seasoned leader or just starting your leadership journey, "The Courage to Command" offers valuable insights and tools to help you make a lasting impact. By embracing the principles outlined in this book, you'll be able to lead with confidence, build stronger relationships, and leave a positive legacy in your personal and professional life.

www.ingramcontent.com/pod-product-compliance
Lightning Source LLC
LaVergne TN
LVHW020509080526
838202LV00057B/6265